The Jews—God's People

Photographs by
Hilla and Max Jacoby

Zondervan Publishing House
Grand Rapids, Michigan

THE JEWS—GOD'S PEOPLE
Originally published in German under the title
DIE JUDEN—GOTTES VOLK.

Copyright © 1983 by Hänssler-Verlag
Neuhausen-Stuttgart, West Germany
English translation © 1984 by The Zondervan Corporation
Grand Rapids, Michigan

Daybreak Books are published by
Zondervan Publishing House
1415 Lake Drive, S.E.,
Grand Rapids, Michigan 49506

Library of Congress Cataloging in Publication Data

Jacoby, Hilla.
    The Jews—God's people.
    Translation of: Die Juden—Gottes Volk.
    1. Israel—Description and travel—Views. 2. Bible.
O.T.—Illustrations. I. Jacoby, Max, 1919–   . II. Title.
DS108.5.J31813 1984   779'.995694   84-7278
ISBN 0-310-42430-5

Printed in the Federal Republic of Germany

Preface

"Behold, I have graven thee upon the palms of my hands . . ." *(Isaiah 49:16).*

I took the photographs in this book together with my wife, Hilla. We were motivated by two facts that are important in my life. First, I was born a Jew. This is neither my "merit" nor my "fault," but God's doing. Second, I have been a photographer all my life. The Lord gave me the ability to perceive visually and the skill to translate experience into pictures. What a marvelous task—to look directly into the faces of the people with whom our Lord made His eternal covenant, as the Bible teaches us. But photography has limitations—it can present the theme of our book only pictorially; it is the Word of the Lord alone that can ultimately explain and present proof. Therefore, we have used portions of the Bible that relate to the theme of our book as the only truly competent text.

Yet I want to add something from the human, and especially from the Jewish, perspective. I believe that every Jew is aware that somehow, something about him or her is "different," although most Jews do not realize what it is that makes a person a Jew. (Until a few years ago this was true also of me.) "To be born a Jew, to die a Jew"—that is the conviction of most of the Jews in the world, regardless of their sufferings, persecutions, and the never-ending anti-Semitism. Ninety-nine percent of all Jews do not want to lose their identity as Jews.

Something about this people must be extraordinary, something that has enabled them to survive attempts to destroy them through the centuries—scattered to the ends of the world, without a home of their own, without their own language (apart from the biblical prayer language, Hebrew).

But in our time the Jews are gathering once again in a tiny but incredibly strong nation. The State of Israel has come into existence! The biblical prophecies, which were given to the people of Israel, are being fulfilled. The rebuilding of Jerusalem has been completed. It was foretold that a strong and beautiful generation would be born in this land and that the land would blossom and bear fruit. The prophet Zechariah says, "I am going to make Jerusalem a cup that causes reeling to all the peoples around . . . and all the nations of the earth shall be gathered against it" (12:2–3 NASB). Fifty years ago Jerusalem was a place of little importance, forgotten by the world, but not by the Jews—from birth they long for the Holy City with a longing that has been passed on from generation to generation in every corner of the world. "Next year in Jerusalem"—that has been their prayer, their longing for two thousand years. This is not sentimentality—it is infinitely more. It is the dormant knowledge that God our heavenly Father "dwells" in Zion, as the Bible declares over and over again. Today, Jerusalem has become a political world center. The Jews have rebuilt her beautifully and are determined to keep Jerusalem as their legitimate and only capital. "A cup that causes reeling to all the peoples around. . ."—how true the Holy Scriptures are!

What God has said in His Word He has fulfilled. The Jewish people would be wise to seek their Creator, Benefactor, Judge, Ever-loving Father, and Lord, "that they might live," as it is written. Our book intends to be a message for those who have open eyes, open ears, and open hearts.

We will be deeply grateful if we will have helped the reader of this book to see a little more clearly, to observe a little more closely, and thus to gain a deeper understanding.

"Hear me, O Judah, and ye inhabitants of Jerusalem. Believe in the LORD your God, so shall ye be established; believe his prophets, so shall ye prosper" *(2 Chronicles 20:20).*

Max Moshe Jacoby

Introduction

Jesus Christ said: "Salvation comes from the Jews" *(John 4:22)*.

It is incomprehensible that during the past two thousand years there have been so many people who called themselves Christians but hated and persecuted the Jews. This is a paradox. Jesus Christ came to the world as a Jew, in accordance with God's plan. He came to bring salvation, in the first place to the Jews. Only later it became clear that His teachings and His sacrifice would bring redemption to Gentiles as well.

His teachings are those of the God of Abraham, Isaac, and Jacob. Furthermore, He made concretely visible the never-ending love of God, who gave His only begotten Son as the purest sacrifice ever (John 3:16) to make atonement for the sins of His chosen people—and in doing so also for the sins of all humanity. He became victorious once and for all over the forces of evil. Now the way leading to God the Father is open. Christians believe that their salvation is in Christ. As His followers they are committed to the same absolute love and obedience toward God out of which He lived. He died on the cross for our sins out of love and of His own free will (John 10:17–18). He who follows Jesus follows the way of love. He who is dominated by hatred does not follow Jesus. "Love your God with all your heart and love your neighbor as yourself!" This is the command of both the Old and New Testaments. If humanity were to obey the God of the Jews (and of the Christians), there would be no wars, famines, ecological problems, fraud, or crimes.

The Jews are not only our neighbors but also our brothers—and above all, they are "the apple of God's eye." Consequently, anyone who hurts the Jews hurts God. All prophecies concerning nations who sinned against the Jewish people have been fulfilled. Once-mighty empires have perished, but the Jews still exist. Where are Assyria and Babylon? Where are the Greek and Roman empires? What about the "Thousand-year Reich" of Hitler? It was shattered, and today a smaller Germany is divided; but even more devastating are her spiritual poverty, her lost souls, the vast majority of her people who live in alienation from God.

The Jews, God's chosen people? Yes, the Bible confirms it in many ways. God calls Israel His "first-born"—granting it a position of privilege. God revealed Himself to all mankind through the Jews: the living God lets us know through His Word how we can and should live with Him. We learn through His Word about His omnipotence, His law, His mighty deeds, and His love. He reveals His own character through the people of the Bible, and through them He shows us the conditions for His mercy and the reasons for His punishments. In God's dealings with the Jews, the Jews stand in for all humanity. Yes, the Jews have been disobedient to God. They have refused to accept the responsibilities and obligations of their privileged position.

But have we, the Gentiles, not been disobedient to God's will? Don't we think we know it better and believe that God made a mistake in this or that situation? Don't we grumble against Him all too often, filled with selfishness, impatience, hypocrisy, immorality, and the desire for power? The Jews are equally as weak, selfish, stubborn, and sinful as the rest of humanity. But through them God shows His everlasting love for all men, but also how He will deal (ultimately on the Judgment Day) with those who are haughty, self-righteous, and indifferent toward Him. Whenever His chosen people followed Him in love and obedience, they were blessed in abundance. The same is true for all humanity. We must decide: Do we follow human reasoning, so important to the world, or do we follow the divine logic that is firmly established in the Bible? The reality of so many fulfilled prophecies stands on the side of the latter.

We Christians should never forget what we owe to the Jews: all that is truly important in our lives. The Bible, written by the Jews, decisively points to the reality of God's existence. The Bible gives us insight into the character of God and into His ways of dealing with humanity. Our most important laws go back to the Ten Commandments, given by God to the Jews, which have had influence and have been accepted worldwide.

God's greatest gift to the whole world is THE KING OF THE JEWS, "YESHUAH HA MASHIACH"—whom the Gentiles call by His Greek name, JESUS CHRIST. The Bible foretells that He will come back at the end of time—back to Israel, to His people. The Bible describes what the world will be like immediately before His return. This description is awesome in its close resemblance to the condition of the world today.

We want to thank
— The Israel Museum (Shrine of the Book), Jerusalem
— The Nahum Goldman Diaspora Museum, Tel Aviv, Beth Hatefuoth (endpaper illustration: Arch of Titus, Rome)
— The Holy Land Hotel, Jerusalem (model of the city of Jerusalem in Herod's time)
— Sculptor Benno Elkan (menorah in front of the Knesset)
— The Avi-Desert-Safari travel bureau in Eilat, which guided us efficiently and pleasantly through the Sinai and provided us with helpful information.

We also thank all those who allowed their pictures to be taken, including those whose pictures were not used. It was difficult to make a choice. Our criterion was not beauty; rather, we attempted to present a panorama of faces in order to show the diversity of characters.

We especially thank those whose pictures are found in this book but whose permission we could not obtain—the people in the snapshots taken in the streets. We trust that these people will understand that authentic "life" can be photographed only if the pictures are taken unnoticed. This is of course especially true of the pictures we took at the Wailing Wall. We are deeply grateful to see in those pictures the gripping and direct evidence of the relationship between the Jewish people and their God. They will agree with us that photos of this kind should not be omitted from a book that bears the title *The Jews—God's People*.

Thank you.

Hilla Jacoby

The Jews—God's People

The Jews—God's People

I will bless them that bless thee, and curse him that curseth thee: and in thee shall all families of the earth be blessed.
(Genesis 12:3)

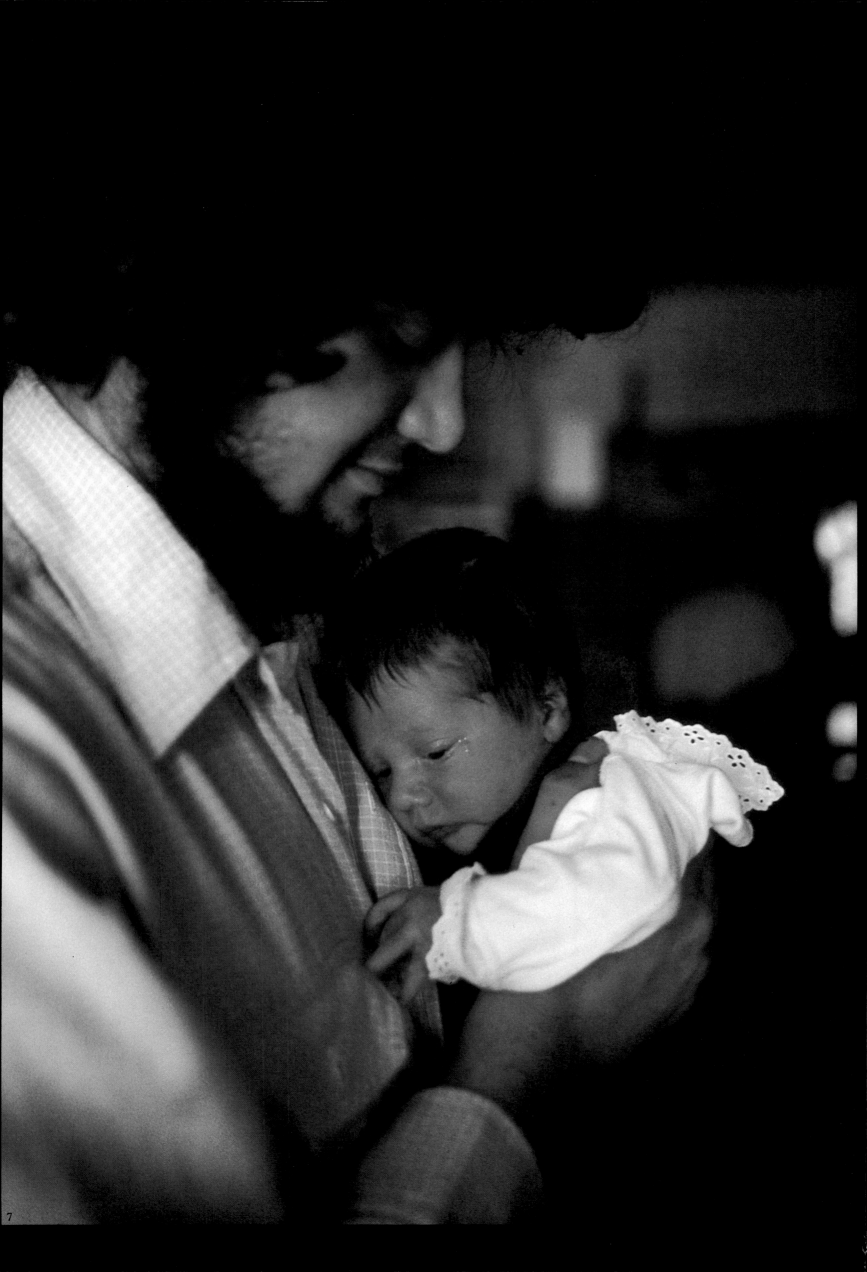

14

15

Thus saith the LORD unto the house of Israel, Seek ye me, and ye shall live.
(Amos 5:4)

20

21

22

If ye shall despise my statutes, or if your soul abhor my judgments, so that ye will not do all my commandments, but that ye break my covenant.... Ye shall have no power to stand before your enemies.... Ye shall perish among the heathen, and the land of your enemies shall eat you up.
Leviticus 26:15, 37–38)

The LORD shall scatter thee among all people, from the one end of the earth even unto the other.... And among these nations shalt thou find no ease,... but the LORD shall give thee there a trembling heart, and failing of eyes, and sorrow of mind: and thy life shall hang in doubt before thee; and thou shalt fear day and night, and shalt have none assurance of thy life.
Deuteronomy 28:64–66)

If they shall confess their iniquity, and the iniquity of their fathers, with their trespass which they trespassed against me, and that also they have walked contrary unto me; and that I also have walked contrary unto them, and have brought them into the land of their enemies; if then their uncircumcised hearts be humbled, and they then accept of the punishment of their iniquity: then will I remember my covenant with Jacob, and also my covenant with Isaac, and also my covenant with Abraham will I remember; and I will remember the land.
Leviticus 26:40–42)

For thou art an holy people unto the LORD thy God: the LORD thy God hath chosen thee to be a special people unto himself, above all people that are upon the face of the earth. The LORD did not set his love upon you, nor choose you, because ye were more in number than any people; for ye were the fewest of all people: but because the LORD loved you, and because he would keep the oath which he had sworn unto your fathers, hath the LORD brought you out with a mighty hand, and redeemed you out of the house of bondmen, from the hand of Pharaoh king of Egypt.
Deuteronomy 7:6–8)

The LORD shall establish thee an holy people unto himself, as he hath sworn unto thee, if thou shalt keep the commandments of the LORD thy God, and walk in his ways. And all people of the earth shall see that thou art called by the name of the LORD; and they shall be afraid of thee.
(Deuteronomy 28:9-10)

Before all thy people I will do marvels, such as have not been done in all the earth, nor in any nation.
(Exodus 34:10)

And it shall come to pass, when all these things are come upon thee, the blessing and the curse, which I have set before thee, and thou shalt call them to mind among all the nations, whither the LORD thy God hath driven thee, and shalt return unto the LORD thy God, and shalt obey his voice according to all that I command thee this day, thou and thy children, with all thine heart, and with all thy soul; that then the LORD thy God will turn thy captivity, and have compassion upon thee, and will return and gather thee from all the nations whither the LORD thy God hath scattered thee. If any of thine be driven out unto the outmost parts of heaven, from thence will the LORD thy God gather thee, and from thence will he fetch thee: And the Lord thy God will bring thee into the land which thy fathers possessed, and thou shalt possess it; and he will do thee good, and multiply thee above thy fathers. And the LORD thy God will circumcise thine heart, and the heart of thy seed, to love the LORD thy God with all thine heart, and with all thy soul, that thou mayest live. And the LORD thy God will put all these curses upon thine enemies, and on them that hate thee, which persecuted thee.
(Deuteronomy 30:1-7)

I will walk among you, and will be your God, and ye shall be my people.
(Leviticus 26:12)

24
Judea

25
In the Carmel Range

The LORD . . . said unto Abram, Get thee out of thy country, and from thy kindred, and from thy father's house, unto a land that I will shew thee.
(Genesis 12:1)

And in thy seed shall all the nations of the earth be blessed; because thou hast obeyed my voice.
(Genesis 22:18)

26
Salt deposits in the vicinity of the Dead
Sea

27
In the Negev near the Dead Sea. Tradi-
tion claims that this is Lot's wife

28
Abraham's Oak in Mamre

29
Oak grove in Mamre

30
In the vicinity of Hebron

32

33

31
Near Avdat in the Negev

32
Spring near Avdat

33
Abraham's Well in Beersheba

34
In the vicinity of Bethel

35
At Abraham's Grave in Machpelah near Hebron

Thus saith the LORD, . . . Ye shall seek me, and find me, when ye shall search for me with all your heart. (*Jeremiah 29:10, 13*)

The Lord spake unto Moses, Go unto Pharaoh, and
say unto him, Thus saith the LORD, Let my people go

45

45
Rock spring in the Judean Desert

46, 47
In the Sinai Mountains

48
The Sinai Mountains as seen from
Mount Horeb

The LORD went before them by day in a pillar of a cloud, to lead them
the way; and by night in a pillar of fire, to give them light.
(Exodus 13:21)

48

51

49
On the "Mountain of Moses" (Mount Horeb)

50
The Tablets of the Law as depicted on the Menorah of Benno Elkan in front of

54

55

56

O Israel, Fear not: for I have redeemed thee, I have called thee by thy name; thou art mine.... For I am the LORD thy God, the Holy One of Israel, thy Saviour:... every one that is called by my name ... I have created ... for my glory.

(Isaiah 43:1, 3, 7)

58

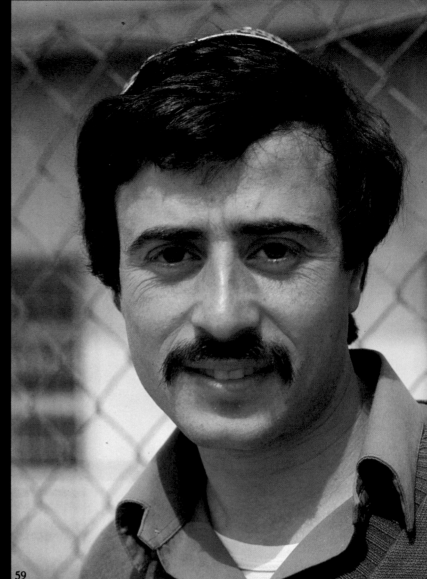

59

61

62

63

65

Then shall ye call upon me, and ye shall go and pray unto me, and I will hearken unto you. . . . And I will be found of you, saith the LORD: and I will turn away your captivity, and I will gather you from all the nations, and from all the places whither I have driven you, saith the LORD.
(Jeremiah 29:12, 14)

66

67

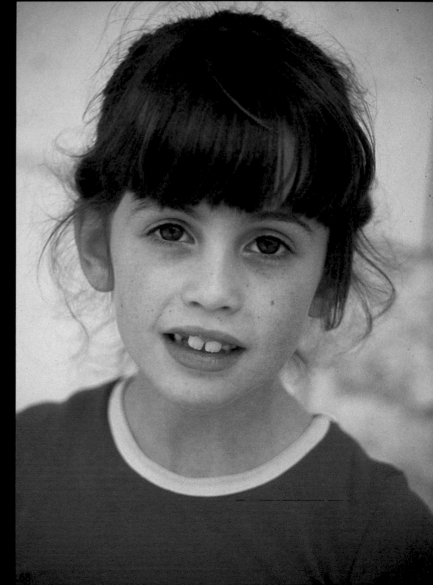

Fear not, . . . I will help thee, saith the LORD, and thy
redeemer, the Holy One of Israel.
(Isaiah 41:14)

The LORD said unto him, This is the land which I sware unto Abraham, unto Isaac, and unto Jacob, saying, I will give it unto thy seed. *(Deuteronomy 34:4)*

73
Date palm

74
Fig tree

75
The Jordan near the Sea of Gennesaret

77

The word of the LORD came to Jeremiah, saying, Considerest thou not what this people have spoken, saying, The two families which the LORD hath chosen, he hath even cast them off? thus they have despised my people, that they should be no more a nation before them. Thus saith the LORD; If my covenant be not with day and night, and if I have not appointed the ordinances of heaven and earth; then will I cast away the seed of Jacob, and David my servant.
(Jeremiah 33:23–26)

78

86

87

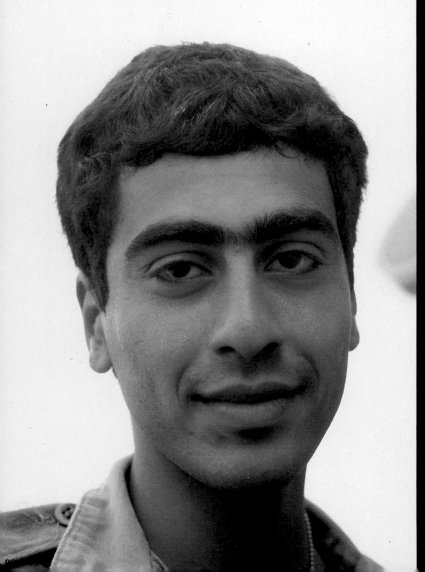

89

90

91

92

One man of you shall chase a thousand: for the LORD your God, he it is that fighteth for you, as he hath promised you. Take good heed therefore unto yourselves, that ye love the LORD your God. (Joshua 23:10–11)

93

93
Mount Gerizim

94

I will appoint a place for my people Israel, and will plant them, that they
may dwell in a place of their own, and move no more; neither shall the
children of wickedness afflict them any more, as beforetime.
(2 Samuel 7:10)

101

100
Well by Samuel's Grave near Gibeon

101
Roman amphitheater in Beit Shean

102
Jerusalem

103
Jerusalem

104
City of David (Jerusalem)

105
The Tower of David, or Citadel, in
Jerusalem

For Zion's sake will I not hold my peace, and for
Jerusalem's sake I will not rest, until the righteousness
thereof go forth as brightness, and the salvation thereof as a lamp that burneth.
(Isaiah 62:1)

106

106
Solomon's pool (water reservoir for
Jerusalem since ancient times)

107
Solomon's copper mines near Eilat

Blessed be the LORD, that hath given rest unto his people Israel, according to all that he promised: there hath not failed one word of all his
good promise, which he promised by the hand of Moses his servant.
(1 Kings 8:56)

You only have I known of all the families of the earth: therefore I will punish you for all your iniquities.
(Amos 3:2)

Surely the Lord GOD will do nothing, but [that] he revealeth his secret unto his servants the prophets.
(Amos 3:7)

Hear ye the word of the LORD, O house of Jacob, and all the families of the house of Israel: . . . What iniquity have your fathers found in me, that they are gone far from me, and have walked after vanity, and are become vain? . . . And I brought you into a plentiful country, to eat the fruit thereof and the goodness thereof; but when ye entered, ye defiled my land, and made mine heritage an abomination. The priests said not, Where is the LORD? and they that handle the law knew me not: the [rulers] also transgressed against me, and the prophets prophesied by Baal, and walked after things that do not profit. Wherefore I will yet plead with you, saith the LORD, and with your children's children will I plead. . . . My people have changed their glory for that which doth not profit. . . . they have forsaken me the fountain of living waters, and hewed them out cisterns, broken cisterns, that can hold no water. . . . Of old time I have broken thy yoke, and burst thy bands; and thou saidst, I will not transgress; when upon every high hill and under every green tree thou wanderest, playing the harlot. . . . Wherefore will ye plead with me? ye all have transgressed against me. . . . I will plead with thee, because thou sayest, I have not sinned. . . . Turn, O backsliding children, saith the LORD. . . .

At that time they shall call Jerusalem the throne of the LORD; and all the nations shall be gathered unto it, to the name of the LORD, to Jerusalem: neither shall they walk any more after the imagination of their evil heart. In those days the house of Judah shall walk with the house of Israel, and they shall come together out of the land of the north to the land that I have given for an inheritance unto your fathers.
(Jeremiah 2 and 3)

The LORD delighteth in thee, and thy land shall be married.
(Isaiah 62:4)

110

111

116

117

118

119

120

121

122

123

124

125

126

108
All that remains of Solomon's temple: the west wall, better know as the Wailing Wall

109–127
At the Wailing Wall

128
Many Jews put pieces of paper on which they have written their heart's desire into the seams of the temple wall, in the hope that God will fulfill their wish

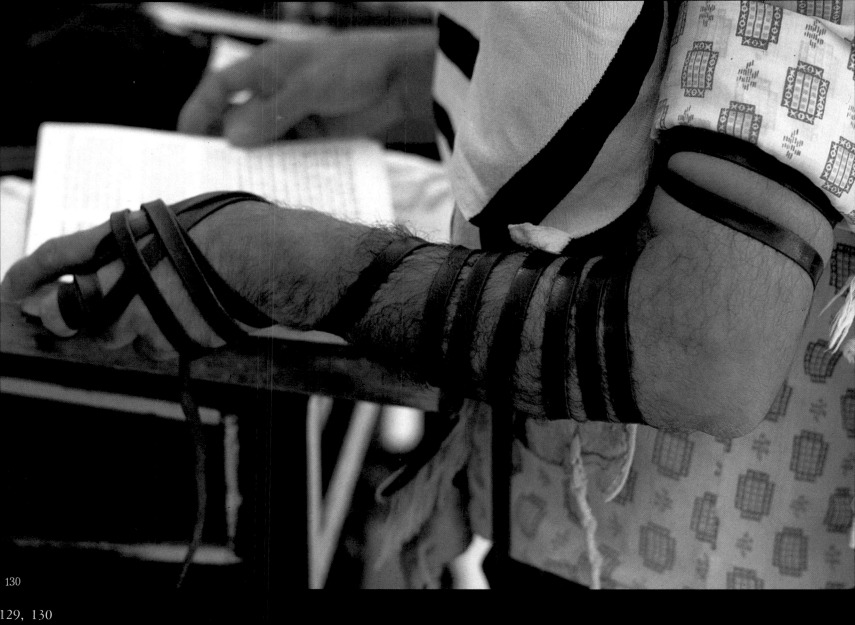

130

129, 130
Pious Jews, praying at the Wailing Wall.
They wear God's Law on their fore-

132

131, 132
Pious Jews at the Wailing Wall, wearing
the traditional prayer shawl

133–135
Bar Mitzva at the Wailing Wall

133
The boy receives the tefillin (prayer
straps)

135
With pride, joy, and reverence, the
Torah is carried to the celebration

And the word of the LORD came to Solomon, saying, . . . If thou wilt walk
in my statutes, and execute my judgments, and keep all my commandments to walk in them then will I perform my word with thee, which I
spake unto David thy father: and I will dwell among the children of
Israel, and will not forsake my people Israel.
(1 Kings 6:11–13)

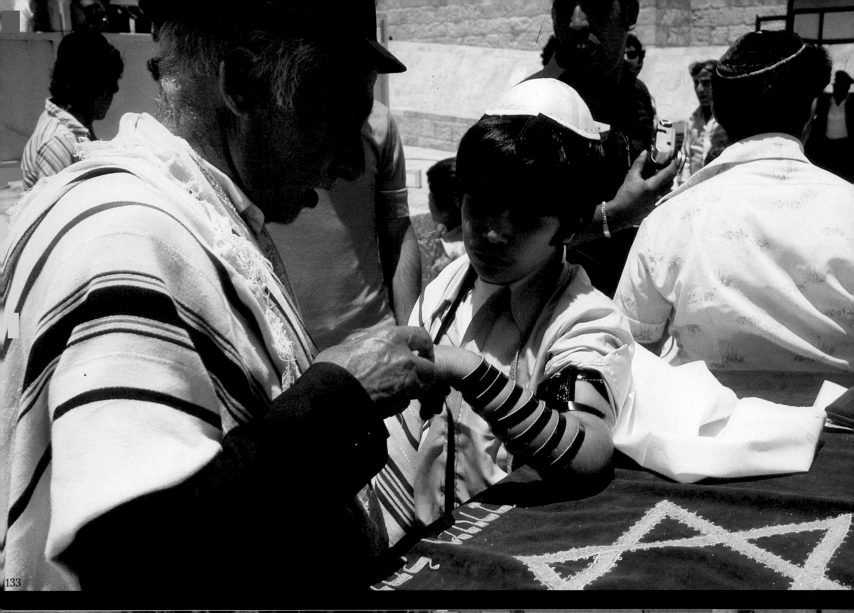

133

134

I will make a covenant of peace with them; it shall be an everlasting covenant with them: and I will place them, and multiply them, and will set my sanctuary in the midst of them for evermore.
(Ezekiel 37:26)

I will be their God, and they shall be my people. And the heathen shall know that I the LORD do sanctify Israel, when my sanctuary shall be in the midst of them for evermore.
(Ezekiel 37:27–28)

I have loved thee with an everlasting love: therefore with lovingkindness have I drawn thee. Again I will build thee, and thou shalt be built, O virgin of Israel. . . . for I am a father to Israel, and Ephraim is my firstborn. Hear the word of the LORD, O ye nations, and declare it in the isles afar off, and say, He that scattered Israel will gather him, and keep him, as a shepherd doth his flock.
(Jeremiah 31:3–4, 9–10)

In those days, and at that time, will I cause the Branch of righteousness to grow up unto David; and he shall execute judgment and righteousness in the land. In those days shall Judah be saved, and Jerusalem shall dwell safely: and this is the name wherewith she shall be called, The LORD our righteousness.
(Jeremiah 33:15–16)

The people that walked in darkness have seen a great light.
(Isaiah 9:2)

Therefore the Lord himself shall give you a sign; Behold, a virgin shall conceive, and bear a son, and shall call his name Immanuel.
(Isaiah 7:14)

For unto us a child is born, unto us a son is given: and the government shall be upon his shoulder: and his name shall be called Wonderful, Counsellor, The mighty God, The everlasting Father, The Prince of Peace. Of the increase of his government and peace there shall be no end, upon the throne of David, and upon his kingdom, to order it, and to establish it with judgment and with justice from henceforth even for ever.
(Isaiah 9:6–7)

Behold, my servant shall deal prudently, he shall be exalted and extolled, and be very high. As many were astonied at thee; his visage was so marred more than any man, and his form more than the sons of men.
(Isaiah 52:13–14)

140

136, 137
Ruins of the royal palace in Sebastia,
Israel's second capital (later called
Samaria)

138
The ruins of Ai

139
Section of the ancient Roman road from
the Mediterranean coast to Jerusalem

140
Valley of the Prophets, southwest of
Jerusalem

141
The temple of Herod (detail of the
model of the city of Jerusalem in Herod's time, on display in the Holy Land
Hotel)

142
Parched soil in Judea

143
Floor mosaic in the synagogue of Naaran
near Jericho

Who hath believed our report? and to whom is the arm of the LORD revealed? For he shall grow up before him as a tender plant, and as a root out of a dry ground: he hath no form nor comeliness; and when we shall see him, there is no beauty that we should desire him. He is despised and rejected of men; a man of sorrows, and acquainted with grief: and we hid as it were our faces from him; he was despised, and we esteemed him not.

Surely he hath borne our griefs, and carried our sorrows: yet we did esteem him stricken, smitten of God, and afflicted. But he was wounded for our transgressions, he was bruised for our iniquities: the chastisement of our peace was upon him; and with his stripes we are healed.

All we like sheep have gone astray; we have turned every one to his own way; and the LORD hath laid on him the iniquity of us all. He was oppressed, and he was afflicted, yet he opened not his mouth: he is brought as a lamb to the slaughter, and as a sheep before her shearers is dumb, so he openeth not his mouth. He was taken from prison and from judgment: and who shall declare his generation? for he was cut off out of the land of the living: for the transgression of my people was he stricken. And he made his grave with the wicked, and with the rich in his death; because he had done no violence, neither was any deceit in his mouth.

Yet it pleased the LORD to bruise him; he hath put him to grief: when thou shalt make his soul an offering for sin, he shall see his seed, he shall prolong his days, and the pleasure of the LORD shall prosper in his hand. He shall see the travail of his soul, and shall be satisfied: by his knowledge shall my righteous servant justify many; for he shall bear their iniquities. Therefore will I divide him a portion with the great, and he shall divide the spoil with the strong; because he hath poured out his soul unto death: and he was numbered with the transgressors; and he bare the sin of many, and made intercession for the transgressors.
(Isaiah 53:1–12)

Incline your ear, and come unto me: hear, and your soul shall live; and I will make an everlasting covenant with you, even the sure mercies of David. Behold, I have given him for a witness to the people, a leader and commander to the people. Behold, thou shalt call a nation that thou knowest not, and nations that knew not thee shall run unto thee because of the LORD thy God, and for the Holy One of Israel; for he hath glorified thee.
(Isaiah 55:3–5)

145

144
Root of fig tree near Gibeon

145
Qumran above the Dead Sea. Here the
Dead Sea Scrolls were found, including the oldest manuscript of Isaiah in
existence.

146
The Isaiah Scroll, now in the Shrine of
the Book, Israel Museum, Jerusalem.

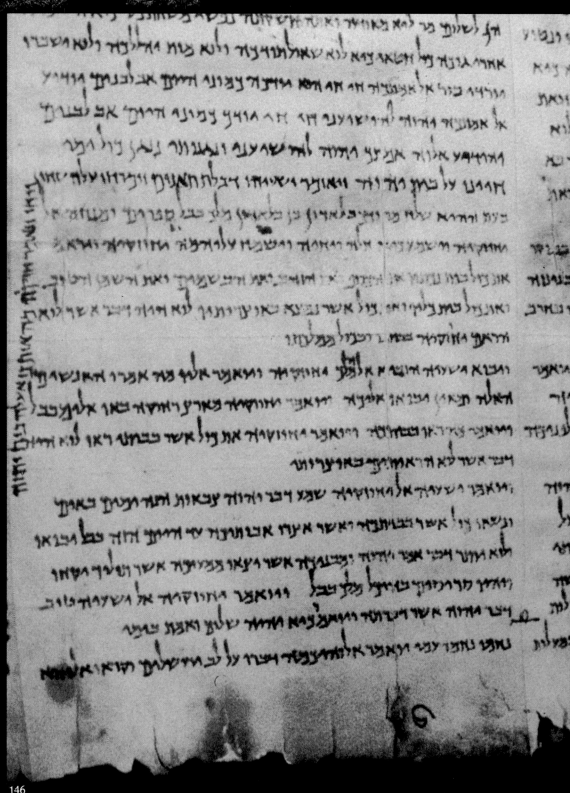

146

My thoughts are not your thoughts, neither are your ways my ways, saith the LORD.
(*Isaiah 55:8*)

I am the good shepherd: the good shepherd giveth his life for the sheep.
(*John 10:11*)

I the LORD have called thee in righteousness, and will hold thine hand, and will keep thee, and give thee for a covenant of the people, for a light of the Gentiles; to open the blind eyes, to bring out the prisoners from the prison, and [those who] sit in darkness out of the prison house.
(*Isaiah 42:6–7*)

149

In the grotto of the Church of the Na-

The word of the LORD also came unto me [Ezekiel], saying, Son of man, thou dwellest in the midst of a rebellious house, which have eyes to see, and see not; they have ears to hear, and hear not: for they are a rebellious house.
(Ezekiel 12:1–2)

O Israel, return unto the LORD thy God; for thou hast fallen by thine iniquity.
(Hosea 14:1)

For as the heavens are higher than the earth, so are my ways higher than your ways, and my thoughts than your thoughts.
(Isaiah 55:9)

Woe unto them that decree unrighteous decrees, and that write grievousness which they have prescribed.
(Isaiah 10:1)

These are the things that ye shall do; Speak ye every man the truth to his neighbour;... let none of you imagine evil in your hearts against his neighbour; and love no false oath: for all these are things that I hate, saith the LORD.
(Zechariah 8:16–17)

For as the girdle cleaveth to the loins of a man, so have I caused to cleave unto me the whole house of Israel and the whole house of Judah, saith the LORD; that they might be unto me for a people, and for a name, and for a praise, and for a glory: but they would not hear.
(Jeremiah 13:11)

Why criest thou for thine affliction? thy sorrow is incurable for the multitude of thine iniquity: because thy sins were increased, I have done these things unto thee. Therefore all they that devour thee shall be devoured; . . . For I will restore health unto thee, and I will heal thee of thy wounds, saith the LORD.

(Jeremiah 30:15–17)

Behold, the days come, saith the LORD, that I will make a new covenant with the house of Israel, and with the house of Judah: not according to the covenant that I made with their fathers in the day that I took them by the hand to bring them out of the land of Egypt; which my covenant they brake, although I was an husband unto them, saith the LORD: But this shall be the covenant that I will make with the house of Israel; After those days, saith the LORD, I will put my law in their inward parts, and write it in their hearts; and will be their God, and they shall be my people. And they shall teach no more every man his neighbour, and every man his brother, saying, Know the LORD; for they shall all know me, from the least of them unto the greatest of them, saith the LORD: for I will forgive their iniquity, and I will remember their sin no more.

(Jeremiah 31:31–34)

Thus saith the Lord GOD; Behold, I am against the shepherds; and I will require my flock at their hand, and cause them to cease from feeding the flock; neither shall the shepherds feed themselves any more; for I will deliver my flock from their mouth, that they may not be meat for them. For thus saith the Lord GOD; Behold, I, even I, will both search my sheep, and seek them out.

(Ezekiel 34:10–11)

151
The Wilderness of Judea

152
The Monastery of the Temptation of
Jesus, near Jericho

And I will set up one shepherd over them, and he shall feed them, even
my servant, David.
(Ezekiel 34:23)

I am the good shepherd, and know my sheep, and am known of mine.
As the Father knoweth me, even so know I the Father: and I lay down
my life for the sheep. And other sheep I have, which are not of this
fold: them also I must bring, and they shall hear my voice; and there
shall be one fold, and one shepherd. Therefore doth my Father love me,
because I lay down my life, that I might take it again. No man taketh it
from me, but I lay it down of myself. . . . This commandment have I
received of my Father.
(John 10:14–18)

154

154
Sculpted representation of the Ark of the Covenant; from the synagogue in Capernaum

155
Fisherman at the Sea of Gennesaret

156
The Golden Gate in Jerusalem

157
Star of David; from the synagogue in Capernaum

158
Olive tree from the time of Jesus in the Garden of Gethsemane

159
Garden tomb in Jerusalem

155

For the people shall dwell in Zion at Jerusalem: thou shalt weep no more:

165

163, 164
Many Jews seek to increase their knowledge of God in the many, well-attended
yeshivot (religious schools) in Israel

165
At the tomb of Rabbi Meir in the synagogue in Tiberias

Ye shall seek me, and find me.
(Jeremiah 29:13)

Call unto me, and I will answer thee, and shew thee great and mighty
things, which thou knowest not.
(Jeremiah 33:3)

166

166
In Mea Shearim, the district of the
Hasidim in Jerusalem

167
Near the Wailing Wall

The LORD also shall roar out of Zion, and utter his voice from Jerusalem; and the heavens and the earth shall shake: but the Lord will be the hope of his people, and the strength of the children of Israel.
(Joel 3:16)

And ye shall know that I am in the midst of Israel, and that I am the LORD your God, and none else: and my people shall never be ashamed.
(Joel 2:27)

Fear thou not, O Jacob my servant, saith the LORD: for I am with thee.
(Jeremiah 46:28)

I will contend with him that contendeth with thee, . . . and all flesh shall know that I the LORD am thy Saviour and thy Redeemer, the mighty One of Jacob.
(Isaiah 49:25–26)

I will pour my spirit upon thy
seed, and my blessing upon thine
offspring.
(Isaiah 44:3)

Behold, I will save my people from the east country, and from the west country; and I will bring them, and they shall dwell in the midst of Jerusalem: and they shall be my people, and I will be their God, in truth and in righteousness.
(*Zechariah 8:7–8*)

And it shall come to pass, that as ye were a curse among the heathen, O house of Judah, and house of Israel; so will I save you, and ye shall be a blessing. . . . As I thought to punish you, when your fathers provoked me to wrath, saith the LORD of hosts, and I repented not: so again have I thought in these days to do well unto Jerusalem and to the house of

Behold, I will gather them out of all countries, whither I have driven them in mine anger, and in my fury, and in great wrath; and I will bring them again unto this place, and I will cause them to dwell safely: and they shall be my people, and I will be their God: and I will give them one heart, and one way, that they may fear me for ever, for the good of them, and of their children after them: and I will make an everlasting covenant with them, that I will not turn away from them, to do them good; but I will put my fear in their hearts, that they shall not depart from me. Yea, I will rejoice over them to do them good, and I will plant them in this land assuredly with my whole heart and with my whole soul. For thus saith the LORD; Like as I have brought all this great evil upon this people, so will I bring upon them all the good that I have promised them.
(Jeremiah 32:37–42)

For I will restore health unto thee, and I will heal thee of thy wounds.
(Jeremiah 30:17)

Behold, the LORD hath proclaimed unto the end of the world, Say ye to the daughter of Zion, Behold, thy salvation cometh; behold, his reward is with him, and his work before him. And they shall call them, The holy people, The redeemed of the LORD.
(Isaiah 62:11–12)

And there shall be no more a pricking brier unto the house of Israel, nor any grieving thorn of all that are round about them, that despised them; and they shall know that I am the Lord GOD. Thus saith the Lord GOD; When I shall have gathered the house of Israel from the people among whom they are scattered, and shall be sanctified in them in the sight of the heathen, then shall they dwell in their land that I have given to my servant Jacob. And they shall dwell safely therein, and shall build houses, and plant vineyards; yea, they shall dwell with confidence, when I have executed judgments upon all those that despise them round about them; and they shall know that I am the LORD their God.
(Ezekiel 28:24–26)

And it shall come to pass in that day, that I will seek to destroy all the nations that come against Jerusalem. And I will pour upon the house of David, and upon the inhabitants of Jerusalem, the spirit of grace and of supplications: and they shall look upon me whom they have pierced, and they shall mourn for him, as one mourneth for his only son, and shall be in bitterness for him, as one that is in bitterness for his firstborn.
(Zechariah 12:9–10)

In that day there shall be a fountain opened to the house of David and to the inhabitants of Jerusalem for sin and for uncleanness.
(Zechariah 13:1)

185
Jerusalem as seen from the old cemetery on the Mount of Olives

186
Jerusalem viewed from Mount Scopus

187
Mount Zion

188
Modern housing along the road from Jerusalem to Gibeon

189
Teddy Kollek, mayor of Jerusalem

190
East Talpiot, Jerusalem

Behold, I will make Jerusalem a cup of trembling unto all the people round about, when they shall be in the siege both against Judah and against Jerusalem.

And in that day will I make Jerusalem a burdensome stone for all people: all that burden themselves with it shall be cut in pieces, though all the people of the earth be gathered together against it. . . . Jerusalem shall be inhabited again in her own place, even in Jerusalem.
(Zechariah 12:2–3, 6)

For the LORD shall comfort Zion: he will comfort all her waste places; and he will make her wilderness like Eden, and her desert like the garden of the LORD.

193

191, 192
In the Valley of Sorek

196

197

198

Thus saith the LORD of hosts; In
those days it shall come to pass,
that ten men shall take hold out of
all languages of the nations, even
shall take hold of the skirt of him
that is a Jew, saying, We will go
with you: for we have heard that
God is with you.
(Zechariah 8:23)

Hearken unto me, ye [stubborn in heart], that are far from righteousness:
I bring near my righteousness; it shall not be far off, and my salvation
shall not tarry: and I will place salvation in Zion for Israel my glory.
(Isaiah 46:12–13)

I will bring them again to place them; for I have mercy upon them: and
they shall be as though I had not cast them off: for I am the LORD their
God, and will hear them.
(Zechariah 10:6)

205

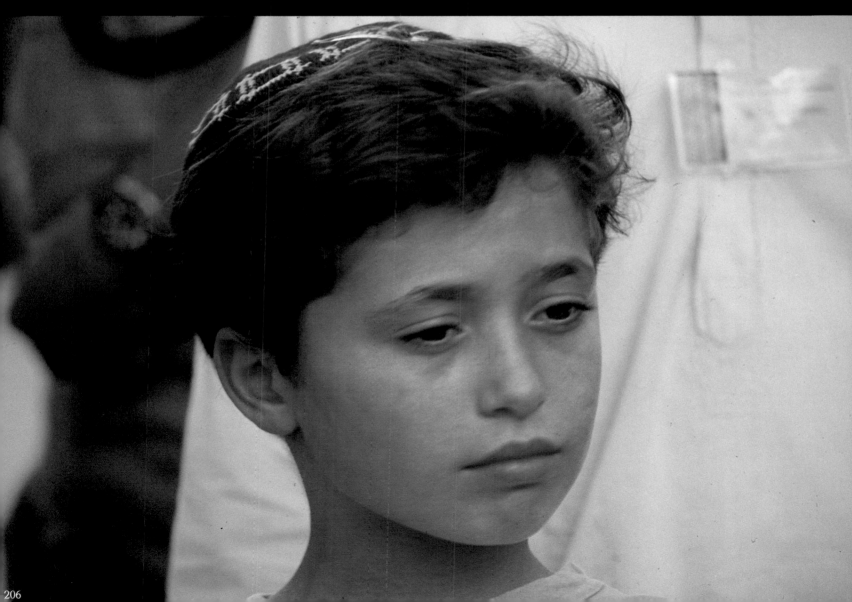

206

208

207
Street market in Tiberius

208, 209
Market in Jerusalem

209

211

212

213

217

218

210–218
In Mea Shearim, Jerusalem

219, 220
In Jerusalem

221
Modern yeshiva near Etzion

I will strengthen them in the LORD; and they shall walk up and down in his name.
(*Zechariah 10:12*)

221

222

224

225

The LORD shall make thee the head, and not the tail; and thou shalt be above only, and thou shalt not be beneath; if that thou hearken unto the commandments of the LORD thy God, which I command thee this day, to observe and to do them.
(Deuteronomy 28:13)

For it shall come to pass in that
day, saith the LORD of hosts, that I
will break his yoke from off thy
neck, and will burst thy bonds, and
strangers shall no more [enslave
them]: but they shall serve the
LORD their God, and David their
king, whom I will raise up unto
them. Therefore fear thou not, O
my servant Jacob, saith the LORD.
(Jeremiah 30:8–10)

227

227
Purim feast in Jerusalem

228
Israeli folk dancers

229
On the Temple Square

Thus saith the LORD of hosts; I was jealous for Zion
with great jealousy, and I was jealous for her with
great fury.... I am returned unto Zion, and will
dwell in the midst of Jerusalem:... Thus saith the
LORD of hosts: There shall yet old men and old wom-

What one nation in the earth is like thy people Israel, whom God went to redeem to be his own people, to make thee a name [by great and terrible things]?
(1 Chronicles 17:21)

How shall I give thee up, Ephraim? how shall I deliver thee, Israel?
(Hosea 11:8)

And I will betroth thee unto me for ever; yea, I will betroth thee unto me in righteousness, and in [justice], and in lovingkindness, and in mercies. I will even betroth thee unto me in faithfulness: and thou shalt know the LORD. And it shall come to pass in that day, I will hear, saith the LORD.
(Hosea 2:19–21)

232

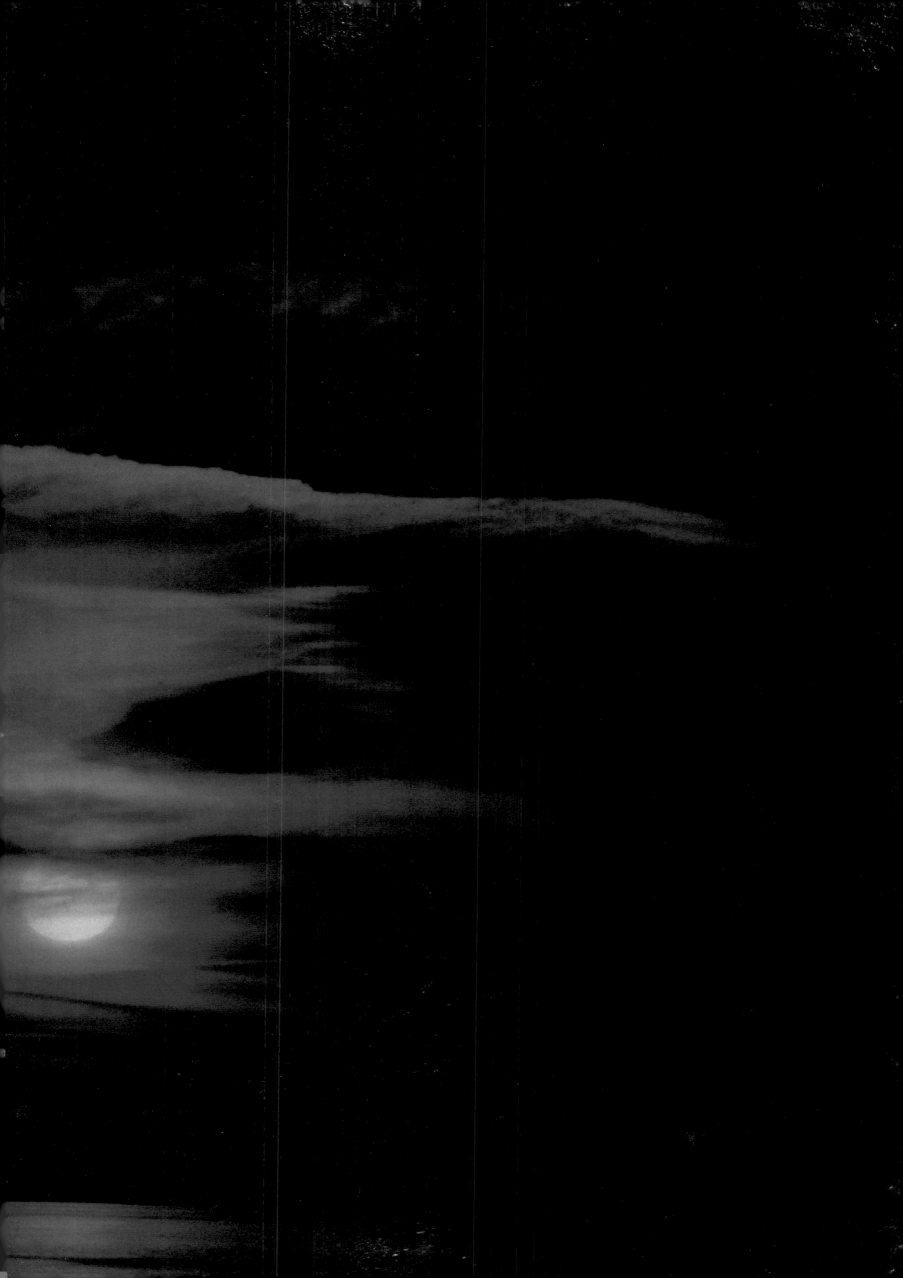

I [Paul] say then, Hath God cast away his people? God forbid. For I also am an Israelite, of the seed of Abraham, of the tribe of Benjamin. God hath not cast away his people which he foreknew. Wot ye not what the scripture saith of Elias? how he maketh intercession to God against Israel, saying, Lord, they have killed thy prophets, and digged down thine altars; and I am left alone, and they seek my life. But what saith the answer of God unto him? I have reserved to myself seven thousand men, who have not bowed the knee to the image of Baal. Even so then at this present time also there is a remnant according to the election of grace. And if by grace, then is it no more of works: otherwise grace is no more grace. But if it be of works, then is it no more grace: otherwise work is no more work. What then? Israel hath not obtained that which he seeketh for; but the election hath obtained it, and the rest were blinded (according as it is written, God hath given them the spirit of slumber, eyes that they should not see, and ears that they should not hear;) unto this day. . . . I say then, Have they stumbled that they should fall? God forbid: but rather through their fall salvation is come unto the Gentiles, for to provoke them to jealousy. Now if the fall of them be the riches of the world, and the diminishing of them the riches of the Gentiles; how much more their fulness? For I speak to you Gentiles, inasmuch as I am the apostle of the Gentiles, I magnify mine office: if by any means I may provoke to emulation them which are my flesh, and might save some of them. For if the casting away of them be the reconciling of the world, what shall the receiving of them be, but life from the dead? For if the firstfruit be holy, the lump is also holy: and if the root be holy, so are the branches. And if some of the branches be broken off, and thou, being a wild olive tree, wert [grafted] in among them, and with them partakest of the root and fatness of the olive tree; boast not against the branches. But if thou boast, thou bearest not the root, but the root thee.

Thou wilt say then, The branches were broken off, that I might be [grafted] in. Well; because of unbelief they were broken off, and thou standest by faith. Be not highminded, but fear: if God spared not the natural branches, take heed lest he also spare not thee. Behold therefore the goodness and severity of God: on them which fell, severity; but toward thee, goodness, if thou continue in his goodness: otherwise thou also shalt be cut off. And they also, if they abide not still in unbelief, shall be [grafted] in: for God is able to [graft] them in again. For if thou wert cut out of the olive tree which is wild by nature, and wert [grafted] contrary to nature into a good olive tree: how much more shall these, which be the natural branches, be [grafted] into their own olive tree?

For I would not, brethren, that ye should be ignorant of this mystery, lest ye should be wise in your own conceits; that blindness in part is happened to Israel, until the fulness of the Gentiles be come in. And so all Israel shall be saved: as it is written, There shall come out of Sion the Deliverer, and shall turn away ungodliness from Jacob: for this is my covenant unto them, when I shall take away their sins.

As concerning the gospel, they are enemies for your sakes: but as touching the election, they are beloved for the fathers' sakes. For the gifts and calling of God are without repentance. For as ye in times past have not believed God, yet have now obtained mercy through their unbelief: even so have these also now not believed, that through your mercy they also may obtain mercy. For God hath concluded them all in unbelief, that he might have mercy upon all.

(Romans 11:1–32)

For a small moment have I forsaken thee; but with great mercies will I gather thee.
(Isaiah 54:7)

For I will not contend for ever, neither will I be always wroth: for the spirit should fail before me, and the souls which I have made. For the iniquity of his covetousness was I wroth, and smote him: I hid me, and was wroth, and he went on frowardly in the way of his heart. I have seen his ways, and will heal him: I will lead him also, and restore comforts unto him and to his mourners.
(Isaiah 57:16–18)

I will turn their mourning into joy, and will comfort them, and make them rejoice from their sorrow.
(Jeremiah 31:13)

Technical Data

All photographs were taken with a Nikon 35-mm camera. We have kept our equipment simple. Many of the pictures were taken with the Zoom 80/200-mm. For portraits and faces we generally used an 85-mm lens. We also used a 20-mm and a 35-mm lens, and (less frequently) a standard-focal-length lens.

We used Kodak Ektachrome slide film. Outside we generally used ASA 64 film and in low-light situations ASA 200 film. Where very little light was available we used ASA 400 film, while in artificial light we used ASA 160 Tungsten Light film.

We did not use filters, except for a polarizing filter in special cases where we wanted to achieve color saturation or a dramatic sky. We do not use a tripod. We generally use the Nikon auto film winder.

All photographs were taken in Israel. Those photographed were asked beforehand whether they were Jews. The scenes at the temple wall, in the streets, and in the marketplaces show probably only Jews. In two pictures Arabs can be seen; the reason for inclusion is that their clothing and tools are a visual representation of Old Testament descriptions.